Solitary
Community

Could Community Support
Cut Costs and Issues?

Rev. Mike Wanner

Table Of Contents

Introduction

I have been writing a lot about prisons and realized that a lot of the complexity is rooted in a constant of change which means that reassessment is constantly recessary to attain a viewpoint that is timely. Here is the list of books that I have written recently:

1. *Angel Raphael Speaks Volume 4: Angels, Addicts, Alcoholics & Prisoners - Oh Yeah!*
2. *Angel Raphael Speaks Volume 5:* Prisoners Caring for Alcoholics - Australia In Miniature Projects Intro
3. *Angel Raphael Speaks Volume 6:* Prisoners Caring for Addicts - Australia In Miniature For Addicts
4. *Prison Jobs Now: Providing Care For Addicts And Alcoholics*
5. *Angel Raphael Speaks - Prisons* (A Kindle only book -2013)
6. *Contained Care Communities: Concept*
7. *Australia In Miniature*
8. *Prison Possibilities Dialogue Series: Concept*
9. *Prison Possibilities Dialogue Series: Volume 2 Dialogues*
10. *Prison Possibilities Dialogue Series: Volume 3 Dialogues*
11. *Prison Possibilities Dialogue Series: Volume 4 Dialogues*
12. *Prison Possibilities Dialogue Series: Volume 5 Dialogues*
13. *Prison Possibilities Voluntary Exile: Concept*
14. *Prison Possibilities Correction Coaches: Concept*
15. *Prison Possibilities for Mexicans: Is A Boat Better than A Wall?*
16. *Prison Possibilities Family Time: A Reason to Thrive!*
17. Prison Genius Pool: *"So Much Genius In Jail"*
18. *Prison Possibilities Access Systems: Prisoner Access by Request*
19. *Prisoner's Lawyers Can Save The American Economy: Make A Buck Doing It & Be Thanked!*
20. *Prisoner Family Talks, Days, Stays & Vacations: Connecting Helps Healing*
21. *Prisoner Writing Projects: Write To Heal, Start Over & Reconnect*
22. *Prison Cell Clearing & Blessing: Clear Entities, Chase Ghosts, and & Create Sacred Space*
23. *Prisoner Professors: Show You Are Aware Create Change With Care*
24. *Prison Reiki? Maybe Someday? A Gateway To Help Heal Prisons & America?*
25. *Judges and An Angel Rule On Possibilities: We Can Cut Sentences & Prison Costs*
26. *Ideas For Prison Wardens: Leadership Is Not Easy*

1 - Why I am Writing This Book

I have been absolutely amazed at the complexity of the whole prison situation and the variety of rules and authorities that oversee the various facilities.

I want to offer some ideas here for consideration. My ideas will probably not be boring but they may be impractical in many facilities because of design differences, regulating authorities and geographical variables.

I intend to fully root this book and all my others in the respect that each individual desires and deserves. Respect for many people is not given because the one who could offer it may lack the understanding of what respect is and how one shows it to other people.

All too often recently, you hear people demand respect and within that demand, they lack respect for the one who they wish to show it to them. You cannot give what you do not have. You might not appreciate it when it is given by others.

When I read about the prisons and the courts and the treatment of prisoners, I am constantly aware of the impersonal nature of the dialogue.

In my experience, a little consideration goes a long way. I invite readers to self test themselves for sensitivity to others.

A good reason to be respectful is because it is the right thing to do. Another awesome reason to do it is that it can be much less stressful and much more productive for all.

2 - Appearances and Perspectives

It is possible to hear people talk about a subject and see little similarity and connection between the viewpoints expressed. The speakers can become infuriated with each others as they appear to listen to the discussion or argument of each other but fail collectively to see the view of the other speaker.

Listening is not complete without understanding of all points and counterpoints of each person as both comprehend each other.

Comprehension can be seen when the other side can exprees your views in their words. Lack of comprehension can lead to circumstances that evolve to ridgid views of an opposer.

Digging in of prisoners and staff may yield more complexity that helps no one. When situations deteriorate further, solitary confinement may be the result.

The words used to describe solitary experiences portray a void of kindness which may be less than motivational and may not be beneficial to the situation or anybody.

Names for Solitary Confinement"

Hotbox,
Hole
Box
Bing
Segregation

Maximum Security
Prison Within a Prison
Administrative Segregation
SHU - Speical Housing Unit
Pound
Block
Cooler
Restrictive Housing
Lockdown
Intensive Management Units

Solitary Could Cause Complications

History seems to have representations that a prisoner alone with just a Bible could repent. Philadelphia has often been referred to as the Quaker City as Quaker ideaology heavily influenced many developments here , I would love to read about success stories that have occurred from this effort but I have not come across any.

I have read that psychiatric disorders could manifest and that seems to make sense because humans by nature are inclined to connect with each other.

3 - The Early Roots of Solitary

I am born and raised in Philadelphia and very proud of the birth of freedom that started here. Recently my research for this book took me to unusual places.

Four years after the American Revolutionary War, the founders of our nation met in Philadelphia to work on what would become the American Constitution and that same year Benjamin Franklin hosted in his house a community group interested in prison reform.

It seems that the Walnut Street Jail located behind Independence Hall had appalling conditions.

A group of concerned citizens called the Philadelphia Society for Alleviating the Miseries of Public Prisons, decided that this must not continue. These discussions influenced events not only in Pennsylvania, but the world over.

Pennsylvania Founder William Penn brought his Quaker values to the new colony. He wanted to avoid the harsh criminal pracrices in much of British North America, where death was the standard punishment for a many crimes.

William Penn was a proponent on imprisonment with hard labor and fines as the treatment for most crimes. Death remained the penalty for murder.

Penn passed in 1718 and conservative groups did away with his Quaker-based system, and returned to harsh penalties that were the norm other places. Jails simply became detention centers for prisoners as they awaited some form of punishment.

Decades passed before change became feasible. Along came a prominent Philadelphia physician Dr. Benjamin Rush with an interest in politics. In 1776, he served in the Second Continental Congress and signed the Declaration of Independence. Later he would lead the push for ratification of the federal Constitution.

It seems that Dr. Rush Felt that crime was a moral disease. He suggested there should be a house of repentence where prisoner could meditate on what they did, experience some spiritual remorse and undergo rehabilitation.

There is a lot in the history books about all this that led up to the construction of the Eastern State Penitentiary. All individual cellblocks in seven wings which radiated out from a central hub.

It opened in 1829 and had central heating, flush toilets and shower baths in each private cell which were very unusual and upscale for the time. Admittees were hooded so they could not even get a perspective of the layout of the buiding. The immates lived in complete isolation with a bible as their only possession.

Sadly, more that 300 prisons throughout the world woud base their design on the Eastern State Penitintiary model.

Charles Dickens visited Eastern State Penitentiary in 1842 and wrote about it in his travelogue, "American Notes for General Circulation."

Dickens' doubt was duly noted. In 1913, Eastern State Penitentiary stopped using the Pennsylvania System of isolation and penitence.

Eastern State Penitentiary deteriorated progressively in the 1960's and was officially closed in 1971.

Today, Eastern State Penitnntiary is a tourist attraction open seven days a week like Alcatraz in California.

At Halloween, the Prison hosts an event that Forbes Magazine described as the "#1 Haunted Attraction in the U.S." Terror Behind The Walls consists of six haunted attractions that create a seamless experience.

4 - Characteristics of Solitary

1. 23 hours a day - time in the small space

2. Cell size about 80 Square Feet, Smaller Than some Horse Stalls. Width 8 feet. Length 10 feet

3. Basic furnishing include a bed, sink and toilet.

4. Exercise time about one hour per day.

5. Loss of freedom.

6. Basic furnishing include a bed, sink and toilet.

7. Exercise time about one hour per day.

5 - Positive Logic That Favors Solitary

A. Solitary provides prisoners a level of protection from the general public

High risk and and dangerous prisoners can be kept segregated with solitary confinement. Security protocols are higher which means prisoner there would be less vulnerable to harm by others.

B. Solitary provides an added level of protection for the public

Protection for the public from serious threats by prisoners is referenced as a justification for solitary.

C. Solitary offers prison safety

Prisoners thought to be a threat to staff or other inmates is referenced as a justification for solitary. Supporters of solitary seems to be adamant that it is needed in order to ensure the majority's safety.

D. Solitary provides prison guards a way to discipline prisoners

Prison guards felt they needed some sort of punishment for negative behavior, because without it, it would be nearly impossible for prison guards to maintain order within the prison walls.

E. Solitary aids in the reformation of prisoner character

Another justification for the criminal justice system discussed is rehabilitation or reformation of character. There seems to be a historic logic for reforming convicts. It was believed that once left alone with their conscience and the Bible, prisoners would reflect on the error of their ways and be changed somehow into law abiding citizens."

F. Solitary satisfies the victims and members of the public that wrong-doers are punished

Interested society members may want to see offenders being punished. That might provide a rationale for solitary confinement, at least when an existing penalty is clearly regarded as "too weak".

6 - Negative Logic Opposing Solitary

A. It creates the loss of freedom.

The loss of freedom can contribute to feelings of increased anxiety, paranoia and claustrophobia. In fact, many prisoners who were in solitary have tried to gain control over their surroundings by resorting to self-destructive behavior.

B. It may not meet all of the prisoner's needs.

Freedom is not usually experienced best when one goes from one contained area to another contained area.

C. Solitary may violate basic human rights.

Solitary confinement can actually fit the definition of torture, as stated in some international human rights treaties. The United Nations Convention Against Torture clearly defines torture as an act through which severe pain and suffering, whether physical or mental, is intentionally inflicted on a person for punishment, intimidation, information or for other reasons, such as discrimination.

D. Solitary offers little to no privacy

Under solitary confinement, guards monitor prisoners during movements of inmates.

E. Solitary might aggravate prisoners personality and mental health disorders

Isolation can contribute to the aggravation of underlyhing patients conditions.

F. Solitary lacks purpose of rehabilitation

The purpose of incarceration systems is offering prisoners the chance to rehabilitate themselves. However, this purpose is lost during solitary confinement, as everything seems to stop except for administrative segregation or short-term protective custody.

7 - Health Effect of Solitary

In many writings about solitary confinement, there are references to health effects which may overlap somewhat. Here is a list of some that I have seen referenced:

Despair
Disorientation
Hallucinations
High Rates of Suicide
Heart Palpations
Excessive Sweating
Insomnia
Back Pain
Joint Pain
Eyesight Deterioration
Poor Appetite
Weight Loss
Diarrhea
Lethargy
Drowsiness
Shaking
Feeling Cold
Aggravation of Chronic Medical Conditions
Anxiety
Depression
Anger
Cognitive Disturbances
Perceptual Distortions
Paranoia and Psychosis

8 - Questions I Have

If I could ask a panel of exerts about solitary, the questions I would ask are:

1. Does the cause of solitary justify the means and the length of solitary?

2. How does the system measure the level of changes and cause dimunation in personal behavior?

3. How can it be known when solitary is no longer necessary?

4. If Solitary does not provide prisoners with an environment that motivates them to change then is it worth it?

5. Is there a better way to mamage interactions between prisoners and staff?

6. Is it possible to have prisoners interact in progressively reactive ways so that mental consequences of isolation can be avoided?

7. Are there Baby Steps To gerate a Rehabilitation Plan?

8. Can There Be a Solitary Plan that expands the prisoner perceptable awareness?

9. Can Solitary Prisoner Experiences be measured?

10. How successful is Solitary for rehabilitation.

9 - Phone Healing Effort

Safety or punishment seem to be the prime motivators for the use of solitary. Health effects that are reported seem to be caused, influenced, complicated by or aligned in unison with the solitary conditions and/or the length of the time the prisoner is in solitary.

Changing up the circustances ever so slightly may offer an opportunity to notice changes incidental to the changing up.

The cheapest and easiest way to offer something new would to install a cheap internal telephone that could be used to see if the prisoner would cooperate even a little bit more than normal.

The suggestion would be to progress very slowly to introduce the idea.

1. A couple weeks before starting, give the prisoner a note indicating that they will be offered an opportunity to connect with someone within the prison. The note could declare the availability once a week of a call to :
> Minister
> Neighboring Cell
> Librarian

2. A week before the effort, another note could announce the date, time and conditions for the call.

10 - Video Healing Effort

Changing up the circustances again ever so slightly may be considered if the Phone Healing Effort offer went well. This effort is another opportunity to offer possible changes incidental to the shifts of prisoners in isolation.

Another cheap and easy way to offer something new would be to install a television or video monitor in a way that the prisoner could watch something while the something being watch is secured in a safe way.

The suggestion would be to progress very slowly to introduce the idea.

1. A couple weeks before starting, give the prisoner a note indicating that they will be offered an opportunity to view something. The note could declare the availability once a week of a brief viewing time to view:
    A Prison Selected video and the title
    A brief Segment of news
    A brief Segment of TV Ministry
    A brief Segment of Therapeutic Suggestions
    A brief Segment of Clinical Patterning

2. A week before the effort, another note could announce the date, time and conditions for the viewing.

11 - Music/Motivational Healing Effort

Changing up the circustances again ever so slightly may be considered if the other Healing Efforts went well. This effort is another opportunity to notice changes incidental to the progress being made.

Another cheap and easy way to offer something new would be to install speakers in a way that the prisoner could listen to something while the something being heard is secured in a safe way.

The suggestion would be to progress very slowly to introduce the idea.

1. A couple weeks before starting, give the prisoner a note indicating that they will be offered an opportunity to hear something. The note could declare the availability once a week of a brief listening time to hear:

     A Prison Selected CD and the title
     A brief Segment of something the prisoner might like
     A Segment of Motivational or Ministerial programing

2. A week before the effort, another note could announce the date, time and conditions for the listening.

12 - Pathway Healing Effort

Changing up the circustances again ever so slightly may be considered if the other Healing Efforts went well. This effort is another opportunity to notice changes incidental to the changing up.

Another way to offer something new would not likely be as cheap and easy as the others would be is to realign the facilities in a way that the prisoner could see and speak to other people in solitary while the others being seen and heard are secured in a safe way.

The suggestion would be to progress very slowly in arranging facilities changes that could be effective to provide the capability. The facility would have to develop a complete plan before any chages are begun.

Depending upon the layouts and constructions of each prison, the cost of such a move could vary widely. It could be as simple as installing windows at an optimal height so that other solitary residents could be seen or seen and heard for controlled periods. Before starting preparatory invitations, it would be wise:

1. A couple weeks before starting, give the prisoner a note indicating that they will be offered an opportunity to see and hear somebody other that their correction officers. The note could declare the availability periodically once a week of a brief interchange amongst the parties and how it would work.

2. A week before the effort, another note could announce the date, time and conditions for the listening.

13 - Visitor Healing Effort

Changing up the circustances again ever so slightly may be considered if the other Healing Efforts went well. This effort is another opportunity to notice changes incidental to the changing up.

Another way to offer something new would be to allow willing visitors who accept personally the risk of visiting the prisoner. It is suggested that a legal waiver be considered by the facility as a prerequisite to the visit.

The suggestion would be to progress very slowly to introduce the idea.

1. A couple weeks before starting, give the prisoner a note indicating that they will be offered an opportunity to visit with the visitor. The note could declare the opportunity subject to all prerequisites

2. A week before the effort, another note could announce the date, time and conditions for the listening.

14 - Prisoner Pow Wow Healing Effort

Changing up the circustances again ever so slightly may be considered if the other Healing Efforts went well. This effort is another opportunity to notice changes incidental to the changing up.

Another way to offer something new would be to allow willing prisoners in the larger facility to visit the solitary prisoners. The prisoner visitors would have to accept personally the risk of visiting the prisoner. It is suggested that a legal waiver be consider by the facility as a prerequisite to the visit.

The suggestion would be to progress very slowly to introduce the idea.

1. A couple weeks before starting, give the prisoner a note indicating that they will be offered an opportunity to visit with the prisoner visitor. The note could declare the opportunity subject to all prerequisites

2. A week before the effort opportunity, another note could announce the date, time and conditions for the listening.

15 - Wrap Up

There may be many questions in the minds of readers so I will endeavor to answer the ones I might expect.

Why Suggest These Things?

Most of what you read about Solitary is rather matter of fact and seems to be absolute answers. A brief intro to the concepts is capsuled in the Pro's and Con's above.

The intensity of the alarming circumstances that trigger the entry in to Solitary seems in language to be quite ridgid and unchangeable and that may be contraproductive for the prisoner, the prison, the staff, the authority that owns or contracts the facilities and of course for the taxpayer. Solitary is much more costly than standard cells.

Over time things are unlikely to improve unless efforts are initiated. Things may be more likely to worsen over time as the health effects can exacerbate behavior, risks to staff and costs.

In the second half of a message in Message Set Nine of the Angel Raphael Speaks series titled "Prison Life of the Future" I channeled "Please consider as if the vibration of a prison existed on a scale that you could read called the love fear continuum. Consider that a single increment move on that scale that went away from fear and moved towards love was actually beneficial to all who passed through the premises.

As you ever so slightly held that thought, you entertained the possibility for a shift for the imprisoned and guards of the

24

future. Congratulations, for you have allowed some light to shine on a subject that is almost perpetually locked in pessimism. "ARS 9

That message was about prisons in general but the reality I think is more intense regarding solitary.

Evaluation

Solitary may be the most costly and risky of the sections within many prisons. Reasonable efforts to provide human kindness would be difficult to criticize if diligence in safety for the staff was increased in the process and crises for the prisoner receiving the kindness stabilized or diminished because the aggravation was less.

There is little here that can be easily quantified and precisely evaluated from a cost standpoint but even if efforts merely prevented cost escalation and prisoner confrontations, the effort would have great value in destressing the facility and providing peaceful sentence serving, a better work environment and perhaps a foundation place from which rehabilitation can bloom for prisoners, the prison staff and all their families.

*

Blessed Be All Who Read These Words, AND SO IT IS!

For
Considering
These
Ideas

Ever

It Does Not Help
Prayer Still Does!

Resource Site http://www.Create-A-Prayer.com

18 - Resource Books

Distant Healing Sessions (or Join Mail List) – Write To mikewann@voicenet.com

Books by Rev. Mike at www.Amazon.com

Veterans Healing Six Pack
1. *Trauma Healing Options for VA Hospitals: Help for Veterans to Own Their Healing and their future.*
2. *Trauma Healing Action Steps for Veterans: Help to Start Healing*
3. *Trauma Healing Action Steps for Veterans: Empowerment*
4. *Trauma Healing Action Steps for Veterans: Forgiveness*
5. *Trauma Healing Action Steps for Veterans: Thought Freedom*
6. *Tea For Veterans: Welcome One Home*

PTSD Power Pack:
1. *The PTSD Project: Turn Pain To Power*
2. *PTSD & Soul Retrieval: Putting One Back Together*
3. *PTSD & The Purple PAD: Calling all Scientists and PTSD Patients*

Angel Raphael Speaks Volume 1: Take Courage! God Has Healing in Store for You!
Angel Raphael Speaks Volume 2: Take Courage! God Has Healing in Store for You!
Angel Raphael Speaks Volume 3: Take Courage! God Has Healing in Store for You!
Angel Raphael Speaks Volume 4: Angels, Addicts, Alcoholics & Prisoners – Oh Yeah!
Angel Raphael Speaks Volume 5: Prisoners Caring for Alcoholics - Australia In Miniature Projects Intro
Angel Raphael Speaks Volume 6: Prisoners Caring for Addicts - Australia In Miniature For Addicts
Reiki Journaling from Japan
Reiki Is Alive: God's Great Gift
Four Parts to Healing
Distant Healing: We Are All Connected
Stress Release Energy Work: How To Cope
Does Reiki Love Heal Cancer?
Group Consciousness
Salute To Philadelphia VA Medical Center: Thank You
Reiki Transcript for Reiki 2 & 3 Channels: Dr. Usui Is That You?
God Bless Kindle & Amazon
Puppies Are Different From People
If Your Dog Dies
Toy Guns Are Obsolete

Great Spirit Made Children With Red Skin: AND
The Cage of Fear: Is Not Locked
God Made Children Red, Yellow, Brown, Black & White: Greet Each Child With Kindness
Emergency Medical Kindness In The Cradle Of Liberty: Big City - Cracked Bell
Angels Are Always Around Addicts and Addicts: Help Is Near Now! Invite It In!
Angels Are Always Around Addicts and Alcoholics: Volume 2 - Tools To Help Re-Light Your Life
Prison Jobs Now: Providing Care For Addicts And Addicts
Controlled Care Communities Concept
Prison Possibilities Dialogue Series: Concept
Prison Possibilities Dialogue Series: Volume 2, 3, 4, 5 Dialogues
Prison Possibilities Voluntary Exile
Prison Possibilities Corrections Coaches
Prison Possibilities For Mexicans: Is A Boat Better Than A Wall?
Prison Possibilities Family Time: A Reason to Thrive!
Prison Genius Pool: "So Much Genius In Jail"
Prison Possibilities Access Control: Prisoner Access by Request
Prisoner's Lawyers Can Save The American Economy: Make A Buck Doing It & Be Thanked!
Prisoner Family Talks, Days, Stays & Vacations: Connecting Helps Healing
Prisoner Writing Projects: Write To Heal, Start Over & Reconnect
Prison Cell Clearing & Blessing: Clear Entities, Chase Ghosts, and & Create Sacred Space
Prisoner Professors: Show You Are Aware Create Change With Care
Prison Reiki? Maybe Someday? A Gateway To Help Heal Prisons & America?
Judges and An Angel Rule On Possibilities: We Can Cut Sentences & Prison Costs
Ideas For Prison Wardens: Leadership Is Not Easy
Solitary Community: Could Community Support Cut Costs and Issues?

Little Books at Kindle.com by Rev. Mike:
English Medical History Questionnaire For Non-English Speakers
English Language Helper For Non-English Speakers
Wise Wonderful Women Are The Well Of The Family
Answers for Test & Research: Dowsing Power
Crisis? Reiki! Baby? Reiki!
Bible References For Healing
Angel Raphael Speaks – Prisons
Angel Raphael Speaks – Veterans
The Saint Off Interstate 95

Angel Raphael Speaks through Rev. Mike Wanner. Please visit
http://www.AngelRaphaelSpeaks.com

19 - Angels Please Prayers

Addict's

Angels of Healing Selected
Help Me to Stay Directed
Come To Me From The Sky
I Am Ready to Succeed Not Try
If I Don't Invite You In
I Might Not Win
I Have Been Lost For Too Long
Help Me To Stay Strong

Alcoholic's

Angels of Healing On High
Help Me to Stay Dry
Come To Me From The Sky
I Am Ready to Succeed Not Try
If I Don't Invite You In
I Might Not Win
I Have Been Lost For Too Long
Help Me To Stay Strong

From

ANGELS ARE ALWAYS
AROUND ADDICTS
AND ALCOHOLICS

HELP IS NEAR NOW!
INVITE IT IN!

REVEREND
MIKE WANNER

http://AngelRaphaelSpeaks.com/AAAAAAA/

20 - Private Channeling

Angel Raphael Speaks is a series of free messages that are channeled through Reverend Mike Wanner for the Highest good and Highest Healing of all concerned.

Many questions arise about Reverend Mike doing private channeling and he does help with that so e-mail him.

Reverend Mike is available world-wide as a psychic channel, emotional release facilitator, spiritual energy practitioner & teacher, and public speaker. He looks forward to meeting you soon!

Email - mikewann@voicenet.com 215-342-1270 PRIVATE SPIRITUAL READINGS/channelings or Spiritual Healing Sessions: Telephone or in person. Rev. Mike is available for private, one-on-one intuitive sessions with you, his Guide Family, and your Guides. He helps by offering clarity on emotional situations about your life, your purpose, your spirituality, and the release of stuffed emotions and cellular memory.
Connect to the love of your Guides today!
Contact Rev. Mike for an appointment.
Sessions available:
Spiritual Readings
Angel Channeling
Distant Reiki Healing
Distant Clearing of Stuffed Emotions
Distant Clearing Cellular Memory
Distant Clearing Energy Blockages
Distant Clearing of the Chakras
Customized needs
Mastermind dowsing responses to yes/no direction finding questions.

Rev. Mike is a facilitator of healing. He brings you and the Divine together so that you can align with the Divine and have a great time and a great life. All healing is between you and God, as it should be. Go ahead and start without Rev. Mike. Visit his prayer site http://www.Create-A-Prayer.com. Take the first step NOW.

21 - Reverend Mike Wanner

Rev. Mike Wanner started his metaphysical and ministerial studies with Reiki in 1993 and has studied seven styles of Reiki in the U.S., Japan, Canada, Denmark and Australia. He is certified to teach. He became certified to teach Integrated Energy Therapy in 1999 and co-taught the first IET class of the new Millennium. Mike began dowsing in 2001.

Ordained as a Metaphysical Minister of the International Metaphysical Ministry and an Interfaith Minister of the Circle of Miracles Ministry, Rev. Mike practices and teaches spiritual energy therapies in the Philadelphia Area.

Rev. Mike holds ministerial degrees from the University of Metaphysics and the University of Sedona. He is a Pastoral Care Associate of Aria - Frankford Hospital. He taught at the National Academy of Massage Therapy and Health Sciences.

Rev. Mike was a faculty member of the Medical Mission Sister's Center for Human Integration's School of Integrated Body/Mind Therapies in Fox Chase, Philadelphia, PA for twelve years.

Rev. Mike is licensed by the teaching of Intuitional Metaphysics to practice Spiritual Healing and Scientific Prayer. Mike is also a Prayer therapist.

Rev. Mike was elected in 2007 to the status of "Fellow of the American Institute of Stress."

In 2008, Rev. Mike became a practitioner of Coincidental Recognition as he incorporated the CoRe System in to his spiritual healing practice.

In 2009, Rev. Mike trademarked a new healing process called Quantum Quatro! Subtle Energy System Support®.

In 2011, Rev. Mike joined the outreach program known as the Health Advantage Group.

In 2012, Rev. Mike became a Certified Professional Coach by The Master Coaching Academy and Joined the Personal Empowerment Group.

Prior to his metaphysical, ministerial and coaching studies, Rev. Mike worked for Sears Roebuck and Co. while in High School and after graduation until he joined the U. S. Air Force in 1965. He returned to Sears from Vietnam in 1969 and stayed until 1978. His final Sears assignment was as an efficiency expert in Methods - Operational Research and Development.

He volunteered with Burholme Emergency Medical Services from 1969 and is still a Life Member and Board of Directors Member. He started a private ambulance company in 1975 and worked professionally in the field until 2001 when he devoted his full attention to real estate investing, healing, coaching and writing.

www.ReverendMikeWanner.com